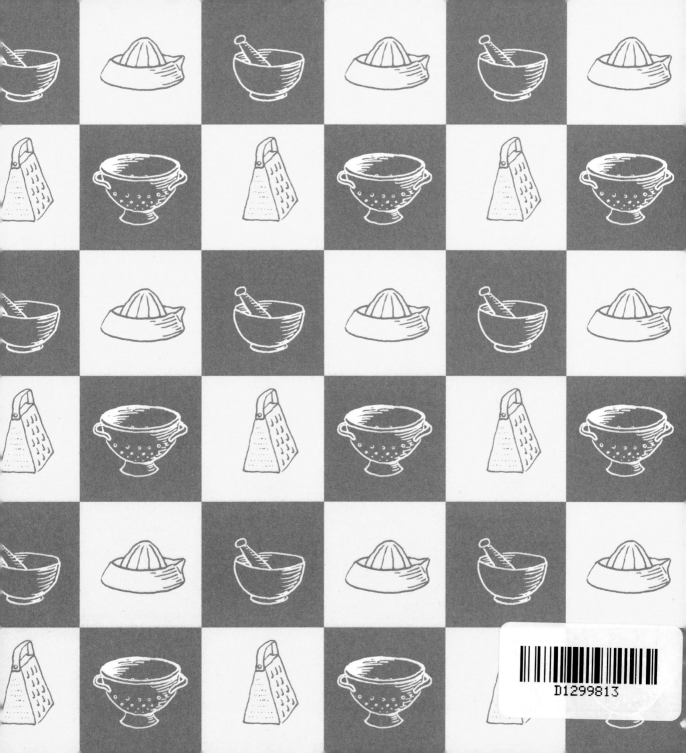

APPLES

APPLES

A Book of Recipes

INTRODUCTION BY SUE LAWRENCE

LORENZ BOOKS
NEW YORK • LONDON • SYDNEY • BATH

This edition published in 1996 by Lorenz Books
an imprint of Anness Publishing Limited
administrative office: 27 West 20th Street
New York, NY 10011

Lorenz Books are available for bulk purchase for sales promotion and for
premium use. For details write or call the Manager of Special Sales,
Lorenz Books, 27 West 20th Street, New York, NY 10011; (212) 807-6739.

Produced by Anness Publishing Limited
1 Boundary Row
London SE1 8HP

ISBN 1 85967 227 2

Publisher Joanna Lorenz
Senior Cookery Editor Linda Fraser
Cookery Editor Anne Hildyard
Designer Lisa Tai
Illustrations Anna Koska
Photographers Karl Adamson, Edward Allwright, Steve Baxter, Michelle Garrett, Nelson Hargreaves,
Amanda Heywood, Tim Hill and Don Last
Recipes Carla Capalbo, Carole Clements, Elizabeth Wolf-Cohen, Norma MacMillan, and Laura Washburn
Food for photography Elizabeth Wolf-Cohen, Frances Cleary, Carole Handslip,
Wendy Lee and Jane Stevenson
Stylists Hilary Guy, Sarah Maxwell, Blake Minton, Kirsty Rawlings and Fiona Tillett
Jacket photography Amanda Heywood

Typeset by MC Typeset Ltd, Rochester, Kent
Printed in Singapore by
Star Standard Industries Pte Ltd

Contents

$\mathscr{I}$NTRODUCTION

We've all been there: about to crunch into a huge, shiny red apple and positively salivating at the prospect. One bite, however, and instead of crisp, juicy flesh and sweet, aromatic taste, it is mealy and devoid of any flavor at all. As far as apples are concerned, size is not important.

In order to select apples which have good, old-fashioned flavor, you should use your nose, not your eyes. When choosing apples – whether it is from a farm stand or the supermarket shelves – apply the smell test. A good apple will have a pleasing, lightly perfumed aroma. The smell and taste of a decent apple can vary from a sweet, juicy Fuji to a tart, crisp Granny Smith. An inferior one – such as many of the imported Golden and Red Delicious – all too often has a grainy texture and virtually no aroma. Apples thrive best in a temperate climate, and there are thousands of varieties to choose from. Just-picked apples can be found at farmers' markets and farm stands.

All through history, apples have played a starring role. From Eve's downfall in the Garden of Eden to present-day Halloween candy apples, they have been associated with providence, tradition and with the fundamentals of life, translated by way of our fruit bowls, resplendent with shiny red, green or yellow apples; and by our every-day desserts – apple pies, tarts and crisps.

One of the most versatile of fruits, they can combine with an astonishing array of flavors; sweet and savory.

This book is divided into five chapters. The recipes begin with salads, soups and dips in the first chapter, the second includes tantalizing ideas such as Somerset Pork with Apples, and Guinea Fowl with Cider and Apples. The next chapter has five variations on apple pie: with strawberries, upside-down Tarte Tatin, lattice-topped Dutch Apple Tart, meringue-peaked tart and the classic apple pie. The hot desserts which follow will have you drooling: choose from Eve's Pudding, Apple and Blackberry Nut Crumble or the wonderfully innovative Apple Couscous Pudding. Finally, cold desserts feature Apple and Hazelnut Shortcake flavored with fresh mint, and a frozen fruit terrine.

Use apples in abundance – to add a sweet yet tangy flavor to your meat, fish and vegetables; and to add a delicious taste to myriad sweet desserts and cakes. This delightful little book will be sure to inspire you with new ideas about how to use our favorite and most versatile of fruits, apples.

Sue Lawrence

$\mathcal{A}$PPLE $\mathcal{V}$ARIETIES

GOLDEN DELICIOUS

Widely available, this variety has yellow skin and pale flesh. Crisp and sweet, it is good eaten raw.

WORCESTER PEARMAIN

This small apple is sweet and is best eaten raw.

FUJI

This apple has greenish-yellow skin with a rosy blush and is sweet and juicy. Excellent in salads.

GRANNY SMITH

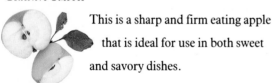

This is a sharp and firm eating apple that is ideal for use in both sweet and savory dishes.

COX'S ORANGE PIPPIN

A fine English dessert apple with yellow, juicy, flesh.

ALKMENE

A recent variety, this sweet eating apple is yellow-skinned with a red blush and has soft-textured flesh.

ROYAL GALA

This red-skinned apple has firm and sweet white flesh. It is excellent for both eating and cooking.

RED DELICIOUS

Well known for its deep red color, it has a tough skin and slightly mealy flesh, and is best eaten raw.

BRAEBURN

A very sweet, juicy and crisp eating apple with a red skin, this can be eaten raw, in salads and sauces.

BRAMLEY

This cooking apple is large, green and acidic in flavor. It is ideal for sauces with savory dishes.

FISHER'S FORTUNE

A crisp dessert apple that is new to the market.

CHARLES ROSS

A juicy new variety that is good for eating raw.

Golden Delicious

Cox's Orange Pippin

Worcester Pearmain

Fuji

Granny Smith

Alkmene

Royal Gala

Red Delicious

Braeburn

Bramley

Charles Ross

Fisher's Fortune

$\mathscr{P}$REPARED $\mathscr{A}$PPLES

Apples seem to have been with us forever and are to be found in all kinds of recipes. Staple fruits that grow well in many parts of the world, apples can be bought fresh, bottled, canned and dried. In any guise their tangy sweetness enhances and complements main ingredients. They feature in a large variety of both sweet and savory recipes, from apple amber to apple salad, from chutney to casseroles and from stuffings to sauces.

DRIED APPLE RINGS AND CHUNKS

To reconstitute, cover in boiling water and leave for

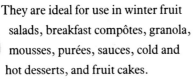

an hour or two then simmer until tender. They are ideal for use in winter fruit salads, breakfast compôtes, granola, mousses, purées, sauces, cold and hot desserts, and fruit cakes.

CHUNKY APPLESAUCE

This can be eaten as a simple dessert with yogurt or cream or used in cooking to make quick sauces, purées, fools, cakes or hot desserts.

GREEN APPLESAUCE

Serve this ready-made applesauce with goose, game, chicken or meat dishes, particularly pork. For a quick dessert, stir into strained plain yogurt.

CANNED APPLE SLICES

These are useful for making pies, tarts or apple cake and are perfect for making quick hot or cold desserts.

APPLE SLICES

Apple slices can be used as a garnish for savory dishes and add an attractive decoration to fresh fruit desserts, mousses or fools.

ROYAL GALA WEDGES

When cut into wedges, this is a delicious apple to eat as a snack or served as part of a fruit platter.

GRANNY SMITH HALF AND QUARTER

These apples are good for cooking because of their firm flesh and sharp flavor. Cut into halves or quarters, and use in apple tarts and cakes.

RED DELICIOUS GARNISH

To make the garnish, cut an apple in half, make a series of V-shaped cuts in the apple, then fan out.

FISHER'S FORTUNE HALF AND QUARTERS

Cut into halves or quarters, it can be served as a quick snack or dessert with slices of cheese.

Apple slices

Royal Gala wedges

Chunky applesauce

Canned apple slices

Granny Smith half
and quarter

Red Delicious garnish

sher's Fortune
half and quarters

Dried apple chunks

Dried apple rings

Green apple sauce

$\mathcal{B}$ASIC $\mathcal{T}$ECHNIQUES

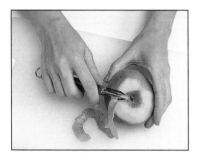

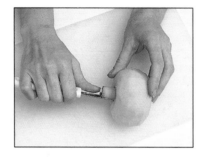

Use a small sharp knife or peeler to remove the skin from the apple. Starting at the top, peel around the apple, turning it as you go, taking off as little as possible.

To remove the core when the apple is to be cooked whole, use an apple corer. Push the corer firmly through the center of the apple and pull it out with the core in it. (If the apple is to be sliced or chopped, you can cut out the core with a knife after quartering it.)

Before slicing or chopping, cut each apple in quarters. Take each quarter and cut into even slices. If the apple is not used immediately, brush the slices with lemon juice to prevent them from discoloring. When preparing apples for applesauce, simply slice or chop them roughly after removing the core.

FREEZER TIPS

Cooked apples are excellent candidates for freezing because they thaw well without significant loss of flavor or texture. They must be prepared for freezing in purée form for sauces, or as ready-made pie filling.

After making the sauce or pie filling, cool completely then spoon into either waxed cartons or ziplock bags. Seal the containers well before freezing.

TIPS AND HINTS

• *Choosing and buying apples*: unlike many other fruits, apples have no off season in the supermarket – they are now available all year round. The varieties you can buy at different times will vary, however. Apples are in abundance in many countries from summer to late winter. If you can't find a particular variety, look for one that is comparable. Farm stands and farmers' markets usually have a good choice of fresh apples.

• *Peeled apples*: if not using them right away, brush them or dip them in lemon juice to prevent the apples from turning brown.

• *Poaching apples*: this method is used when the apple is required to keep its shape in the cooking. Simmer the slices or whole peeled apples gently in syrup in a saucepan for two or three minutes, then turn off the heat and finish the cooking in the residual heat with the lid on.

• *Baking apples*: when baking whole cooking apples, a good way to prevent the skins from bursting in the oven is to score a shallow line in the skin around the circumference of each apple using a sharp knife.

• *Storage of apples*: apples can be stored in many ways, depending on their ultimate usage. If you grow your own or can buy in bulk, eating apples can be stored whole for up to 6 months by wrapping in paper and packing in boxes in a cool, dry place. Remember that they must not be bruised or damaged before storing, and always check them regularly to remove any that have rotted or the rest will spoil.

• *Preserving apples*: apples can be successfully frozen (see Freezer Tips, left) and also make good jams, jellies, chutneys, pickles, and even wine. They are suitable for bottling but since they are more usually preserved by other methods, this is not common. Another method of home preservation is to dry apple rings then store them in jars. Dried apple rings and slices can also be bought from supermarkets and health food stores and soaked before making pie fillings, sauces or simply dropped into casseroles. They make a delicious snack and can also be finely chopped and added to home-made granola.

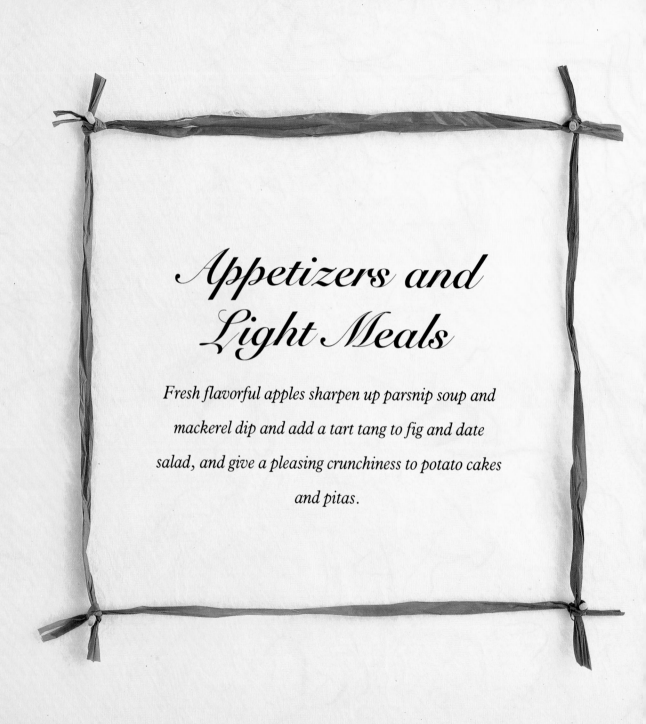

Appetizers and Light Meals

Fresh flavorful apples sharpen up parsnip soup and mackerel dip and add a tart tang to fig and date salad, and give a pleasing crunchiness to potato cakes and pitas.

SMOKED MACKEREL AND APPLE DIP

Serve this quick fish dip with tasty, curried bread dippers.

Serves 6–8

*12 ounces smoked mackerel, skinned
and boned*

*1 eating apple, peeled, cored and cut
into chunks*

⅔ cup ricotta

pinch of paprika or curry powder

salt and ground black pepper

apple slices, to garnish

For the curried dippers

4 slices white bread, crusts removed

2 tablespoons butter, softened

1 teaspoon curry paste

COOK'S TIP

*Instead of using plain, sliced
bread, you could try other
breads for the dippers – Italian
ciabatta, rye bread, or pita
breads would be excellent.*

Place the smoked mackerel in a food processor or blender with the apple, ricotta, and seasonings. Blend for about 2 minutes or until the mixture is really smooth. Check the seasoning, then transfer to a small serving dish and chill. Preheat the oven to 400°F. To make the curried dippers, place the bread on a baking sheet. Blend the butter and curry paste thoroughly, then spread over the bread.

Cook the bread in the oven for about 10 minutes, or until crisp and golden. Cut into fingers and serve, while still warm, with the mackerel dip, garnished with the apple slices.

PARSNIP AND APPLE SOUP

A hearty, warming soup that's excellent served on a cold winter's day.

Serves 8–10

4 tablespoons sweet butter

2 large onions, sliced

1 garlic clove, chopped

2 large parsnips, scrubbed and cubed

2 firm, tart cooking apples (about 1 pound), peeled, cored and cubed

2 teaspoons medium curry powder

6¼ cups chicken broth

1¼ cups light cream

salt and ground black pepper

For the topping

2 tablespoons sweet butter

1 cup pecans, chopped

⅔ cup crème fraîche or sour cream

Heat the butter in a large pan and sauté the onions and garlic over moderate heat until the onions are translucent. Stir in the parsnips and apples and sauté for 3 minutes more, stirring occasionally. Add the curry powder and stir to mix. Cook for 1 minute more. Pour on the broth, bring to a boil, cover the pan and simmer for 20 minutes. Remove from the heat and cool slightly. Pour into a food processor or blender and process until smooth. Return the soup to the pan. Stir in the cream and seasoning and heat gently.

To make the topping, heat the butter in a pan and sauté the pecans over moderate heat for 5 minutes. Serve the soup in bowls topped with the crème fraîche or sour cream and sprinkled with the sautéed pecans.

CHICKEN AND APPLE PITAS

Pitas are great for a teenage party – just supply the ingredients and let the party-goers assemble their own.

Serves 4

¼ red cabbage

1 small red onion, finely sliced

2 radishes, finely sliced

1 red eating apple, peeled, cored
  and grated

1 tablespoon lemon juice

3 tablespoons low-fat sour cream

1 cooked chicken breast (about
  6 ounces), skinned

4 large or 8 small pitas

salt and ground black pepper

chopped fresh parsley, to garnish

COOK'S TIP

*If the filled pitas need to be
made more than an hour in
advance, line the pita breads
with crisp lettuce leaves before
adding the filling. Cover and
chill until required.*

Remove the tough central spine from the cabbage leaves, then finely shred the leaves using a large, sharp knife. Place the shredded cabbage in a large bowl and stir in the onion, radishes, apple, and lemon juice.

Stir the sour cream into the shredded cabbage mixture and season well. Thinly slice the cooked chicken breast and stir into the shredded cabbage mixture until thoroughly coated in the sour cream.

Preheat the broiler. Place the pitas on the broiler pan and toast until warmed. Split them along one edge with a round-ended knife. Spoon the filling into the pitas. Serve immediately garnished with the parsley.

17

FIG, APPLE, AND DATE SALAD

Sweet Mediterranean figs and dates combine especially well with crisp eating apples.

Serves 4

6 large eating apples
juice of ½ lemon
6 ounces fresh dates
1 ounce white marzipan
1 teaspoon orange flower water
4 tablespoons plain yogurt
4 fresh green or purple figs
4 toasted almonds, to garnish

COOK'S TIP

*When buying fresh dates, avoid
any that look shriveled. They
should be plump and shiny,
yellow-red to golden brown and
with smooth skins.*

Core the apples and slice thinly with a sharp knife. Leave the skins on. Cut into fine matchsticks. Place in a bowl and toss with lemon juice.

Remove the pits from the dates and cut the flesh into fine strips, then combine with the apple slices in the bowl.

In a separate bowl, soften the marzipan with orange flower water and combine with the yogurt. Mix together well until smooth.

Divide the apples and dates among the center of four plates. Remove the stem from each of the figs and divide the fruit into quarters without cutting right through the base. Squeeze the base with the thumb and forefinger of each hand to open up the fruit. Place a fig in the center of each salad, spoon in the yogurt filling, and serve garnished with a toasted almond.

STRAW POTATO CAKES WITH APPLE

These potato cakes resemble latkes, *a Central European dish. Work quickly as the potato darkens rapidly.*

Makes about 16

1 tablespoon butter

1–2 eating apples, unpeeled, cored and diced

1 teaspoon lemon juice

2 teaspoons sugar

pinch of cinnamon

¼ cup thick sour cream

Italian parsley, to garnish

For the potato cakes

½ small onion, very finely chopped or grated

2 baking potatoes

oil for frying

salt and ground black pepper

Heat the butter in a frying pan over moderate heat. Add the diced apple and toss to coat. Sprinkle with the lemon juice, sugar, and cinnamon. Cook for 2–3 minutes, stirring, until the apples are just tender and beginning to color. Turn into a bowl.

To make the potato cakes, put the grated onion into a bowl. Grate the potatoes on to a clean dish towel and squeeze the potato dry. Add the potatoes to the onion, and season. Heat ½ inch oil in a large heavy-based frying pan until hot. Drop tablespoonfuls of the potato mixture into the oil in batches. Flatten slightly and fry for 5–6 minutes. Drain on paper towels. Serve each potato cake topped with 1 tablespoon caramelized apple and a little sour cream, garnished with parsley.

Savory Dishes

Crisp, slightly sweet apples are perfect with poultry, and add their tangy taste to a selection of game, lamb, and pork casseroles, pies and vegetable dishes.

SOMERSET PORK WITH APPLES

A rich, country dish using fresh apples and cider.

Serves 4

2 tablespoons butter

1¼ pounds pork loin, cut into
   bite-size pieces

12 baby onions, peeled

2 teaspoons grated lemon rind

1¼ cups hard cider

⅔ cup veal broth

2 eating apples, cored and sliced

3 tablespoons chopped fresh parsley

scant ½ cup whipping cream

salt and ground black pepper

COOK'S TIP

*It is advisable to remove the rind
from the pork before cutting into
pieces. This is best done with
sharp scissors or a sharp knife.*

Heat the butter in a large heavy-based frying pan and sauté the pork in batches until brown. Transfer the pork to a bowl.

Add the onions to the pan, brown lightly, then stir in the lemon rind, cider, and broth and boil for about 3 minutes. Return all the pork to the pan and cook gently for about 25 minutes until the pork is tender.

Stir the apples into the pan and cook for 5 minutes more. Using a slotted spoon, transfer the pork, onions, and apples to a warmed serving dish, cover and keep warm. Add the parsley and stir the cream into the pan and allow to bubble to thicken the sauce slightly. Season, then pour over the pork and serve immediately.

NORMANDY PHEASANT

Cider, apples, and cream make this a rich, flavorful dish – a great change from a plain roast.

Serves 4

2 oven-ready pheasants

1 tablespoon olive oil

2 tablespoons butter

4 tablespoons Calvados or Apple Jack

1⅞ cups hard cider

bouquet garni

*3 crisp eating apples, peeled, cored
    and thickly sliced*

⅔ cup heavy cream

salt and ground black pepper

thyme sprigs, to garnish

Preheat the oven to 325°F. Joint both pheasants into four pieces using a large sharp knife. Discard the backbones and knuckles.

Heat the oil and butter in a large flameproof casserole. Working in two batches, add the pheasant pieces to the casserole and brown them over high heat. Return all the pheasant pieces to the casserole.

Standing well back, pour over the Calvados or Apple Jack and set it alight. When the flames have subsided, pour in the cider, then add the bouquet garni and seasoning and bring to a boil. Cover the casserole and cook in the oven for 50 minutes.

Tuck the apple slices around the pheasant. Cover and cook for about 5–10 minutes, or until the pheasant is tender. Transfer the pheasant and apple to a warmed serving plate. Keep warm.

Remove the bouquet garni, then boil the liquid to reduce the sauce by half until you have a syrupy consistency. Stir in the cream and simmer for 2–3 minutes more until thickened. Taste the sauce and adjust the seasoning if necessary. Spoon the sauce over the pheasant and serve immediately garnished with thyme sprigs.

PORK AND APPLE HOT-POT

An economical and tasty dish using a cheaper cut of pork.

Serves 4

1¼ pounds sparerib pork chops

2 tablespoons sunflower oil

1 large onion, sliced

3 celery stalks, chopped

1 tablespoon chopped fresh sage, or
    1 teaspoon dried

1 tablespoon chopped fresh parsley

2 eating apples, peeled, cored and cut
    into thick wedges

²⁄₃ cup apple juice

²⁄₃ cup broth

1 tablespoon cornstarch

1 pound par-boiled, peeled and
    sliced potatoes

melted butter, to glaze

salt and ground black pepper

sage leaves, to garnish

Remove any bones from the pork and cut the meat into even-size cubes. Sprinkle with seasoning.

Heat the oil in a pan and fry the onion and celery until golden. Remove and place half in the base of a casserole. Arrange the meat on top and sprinkle with half the herbs.

Add the apples and the rest of the onion, celery, and herbs. Season to taste. Blend the apple juice with the broth and cornstarch and pour over.

Preheat the oven to 375°F. Top with the sliced potatoes and brush with melted butter. Cover and cook in the oven for 50–60 minutes, removing the lid for the last 15 minutes to brown the potatoes. Serve immediately, garnished with sage leaves.

LAMB, LEEK, AND APPLE PIE

An innovative combination where lamb and leeks are spiced up with apple.

Serves 4

*1½ pounds lamb neck fillets, cut into
  12 pieces*

4 ounces bacon, diced

1 onion, thinly sliced

12 ounces leeks, sliced

*1 large firm, tart cooking apple (about
  8 ounces), peeled, cored and sliced*

¼–½ teaspoon ground allspice

¼–½ teaspoon grated nutmeg

⅔ cup lamb, beef or vegetable broth

8 ounces ready-made pie pastry

beaten egg or milk, to glaze

salt and ground black pepper

COOK'S TIP

*When you are buying leeks, look
for those that are straight and
well shaped. Avoid any that
have yellow, discolored and
slimy leaves.*

Preheat the oven to 400°F. Layer the meats, onion, leeks, and apple in a 3¾-cup pie dish, sprinkling in the spices and seasoning as you go. Pour in the broth.

On a lightly floured surface, roll out the pastry to ¾ inch larger than the top of the pie dish. Cut a narrow strip from around the pastry, fit it around the dampened rim of the dish, then brush with water.

Lay the pastry over the filling, and press the edges together to seal them. Brush the top with beaten egg or milk, and make a hole in the center.

Bake the pie for 20 minutes, then reduce the oven temperature to 350°F and continue to bake for 1–1¼ hours, covering the pie with foil if the pastry begins to become too brown. Serve immediately.

GUINEA HEN WITH CIDER AND APPLES

Guinea hens are farmed, so they are available quite frequently in supermarkets, usually fresh. Their flavor is reminiscent of an old-fashioned chicken – not really gamey, but they do have slightly darker meat.

Serves 4

4–4½-pound guinea hen

1 onion, halved

3 celery stalks

3 bay leaves

a little butter

1¼ cups hard cider

⅔ cup chicken broth

2 small firm, tart cooking apples (about 1 pound), peeled and sliced

4 tablespoons thick heavy cream

a few sage leaves, plus extra to garnish

2 tablespoons chopped fresh parsley

salt and ground black pepper

If the guinea hen is packed with its giblets, put them in a pan with water to cover, add half the onion, a stalk of celery, a bay leaf and seasoning. Bring to a boil and simmer for about 30 minutes, or until you have about ⅔ cup well-flavored stock. Use this in the recipe instead of the chicken broth.

Preheat the oven to 375°F. Wash and wipe dry the bird and place the remaining onion half and a tablespoon of butter inside the body cavity. Place the guinea hen in a roasting dish, sprinkle with seasoning, and dot with a few pieces of butter.

Pour the cider and chicken broth or homemade stock into the dish and cover with a lid or foil. Bake in the oven for 25 minutes per pound, basting the bird occasionally.

Uncover for the last 20 minutes and baste well again. Slice the remaining celery and add it together with the prepared apples. When the guinea hen is cooked, transfer it to a warm serving dish and keep warm. Remove the apples and celery with a slotted spoon and set aside.

Boil the liquid rapidly to reduce to about ⅔ cup. Stir in the cream, seasoning, and the sage leaves, and cook for a few minutes more to reduce slightly. Return the apples to this pan with the parsley and warm through. Serve with or around the bird, garnished with sage leaves.

APPLE, ONION, AND GRUYÈRE TART

Serve this tart with baked potatoes for a more filling meal.

Serves 4–6

1 large onion, finely chopped

2 tablespoons butter

1 large or 2 small eating apples,
* peeled and grated*

2 eggs

²/₃ cup heavy cream

¼ teaspoon dried mixed herbs

½ teaspoon dry mustard

4 ounces Gruyère cheese

salt and ground black pepper

green salad leaves, to serve

For the pastry

2 cups flour

¼ teaspoon dry mustard

6 tablespoons soft margarine

6 tablespoons Gruyère cheese,
* finely grated*

COOK'S TIP

Instead of Gruyère, try Cheddar
or Emmenthaler cheese.

For the pastry, sift the flour, a pinch of salt, and the mustard into a bowl. Rub in the margarine and cheese, add 2 tablespoons water and form into a ball. Chill. Cook the onion in the butter for 10 minutes until softened. Stir in the apple and cook for 2–3 minutes. Let cool. Roll out the pastry and line a lightly greased 8-inch fluted quiche pan. Chill for 20 minutes. Preheat the oven to 400°F. Line the pastry with wax paper and fill with baking beans. Bake for 20 minutes. Beat together the eggs, cream, herbs, seasoning, and mustard. Grate three-quarters of the cheese and stir into this mixture. Slice the remaining cheese. When the pastry is cooked, remove the paper and beans, add the onion mixture and pour in the egg mixture. Arrange the sliced cheese on top. Turn the oven down to 375°F. Bake the tart for 20 minutes, until golden and just firm. Serve hot or warm with green salad leaves.

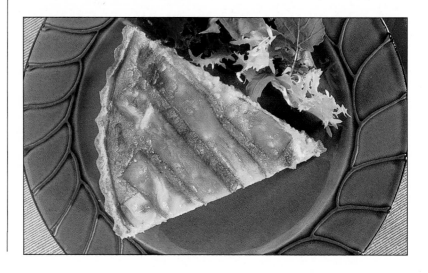

BRAISED RED CABBAGE WITH APPLES

The combination of red wine vinegar and sugar gives this dish a sweet, yet tart flavor. In France it is often served with game, but it is also delicious with pork, duck, or cold sliced meats.

Serves 6–8

2 tablespoons vegetable oil

2 onions, thinly sliced

2 eating apples, peeled, cored and
   thinly sliced

1 red cabbage (about 2–2½ pounds),
   trimmed, cored, halved and
   thinly sliced

4 tablespoons red wine vinegar

1–2 tablespoons sugar

¼ teaspoon ground cloves

1–2 teaspoons mustard seeds

⅓ cup raisins or currants

about ½ cup red wine or water

1–2 tablespoons redcurrant
   jelly (optional)

salt and ground black pepper

Heat the oil in a large heavy-based pan or flameproof casserole and cook the onions over medium heat until golden. Stir in the apples and cook, stirring, for 2–3 minutes more until they are just softened.

Add the cabbage, red wine vinegar, sugar, cloves, mustard seeds, raisins or currants, red wine or water, and seasoning. Stir until well mixed. Bring to a boil over a medium-high heat, stirring occasionally.

Cover and cook over a medium-low heat for about 35–40 minutes until the cabbage is tender and the liquid is just absorbed, stirring occasionally. Add a little more red wine or water if the pan boils dry before the cabbage is tender. Just before serving, stir in the redcurrant jelly, if using, to sweeten and glaze the cabbage.

Sweet Pastries and Cakes

Sharp, flavorful apples make a perfect contrast to light,

crisp pastry in classic pies and tarts, and when combined

with other fruits, make a tangy addition to a selection

of deliciously moist cakes.

STRAWBERRY AND APPLE TART

A dish for lovers – apples and strawberries in perfect harmony.

Serves 4–6

2 firm, tart cooking apples (about
1 pound), peeled, cored and sliced

2 cups strawberries, halved

4 tablespoons sugar

1 tablespoon cornstarch

For the pastry

1¼ cups self-rising flour

⅔ cup oatmeal

4 tablespoons sunflower margarine

COOK'S TIP

It is best to prepare apples just
before you use them. If you do
prepare them ahead, place the
cut pieces in a bowl of lemony
cold water to prevent them
from browning.

Preheat the oven to 400°F. For the pastry, mix the flour and oatmeal in a bowl and rub in the margarine evenly. Stir in cold water to bind and form into a ball. Knead lightly until smooth. On a lightly-floured surface, roll out the pastry and line a 9-inch loose-based tart pan. Trim the edges, prick the base, line the pastry with wax paper and fill with baking beans. Roll out the trimmings and stamp out heart shapes using a cookie cutter. Bake for 10 minutes, remove the paper and beans, and bake for 10–15 minutes or until golden brown. Bake the hearts until golden. Place the apples in a pan with the strawberries, sugar, and cornstarch. Cover and cook gently, stirring, until the fruit is just tender. Spoon into the pastry shell and serve decorated with the pastry hearts.

APPLE PIE

A comforting dish that will take you back to your childhood.

Serves 8

4 firm, tart cooking apples (about
* 2 pounds), sliced*

1 tablespoon fresh lemon juice

1 teaspoon vanilla extract

½ cup sugar

½ teaspoon ground cinnamon

1½ tablespoons butter or margarine

1 egg yolk

2 teaspoons whipping cream

For the pastry

2 cups flour

1 teaspoon salt

¾ cup shortening

4–5 tablespoons ice water

1 tablespoon quick-cooking tapioca

Preheat the oven to 450°F. To make the pastry, sift the flour and salt into a bowl. Rub in the shortening until the mixture forms soft crumbs. Add the water, a tablespoon at a time, and bring together into a ball.

Cut the dough in half and shape each half into another ball. On a lightly floured surface, roll out one of the balls to a circle about 12 inches in diameter.

Line a lightly greased 9-inch pie pan, easing the dough in and being careful not to stretch it. Trim the edges carefully and keep the excess pastry for later. Sprinkle the tapioca evenly over the base of the pastry shell.

Roll out the remaining pastry to ⅛ inch thick and cut out eight large leaf shapes with a sharp knife. Cut the trimmings into enough smaller leaves to decorate the edges of the pie. Score the leaves with the back of a knife to make the leaf veins.

To make the filling, mix together the apples, lemon juice, vanilla extract, sugar, and cinnamon. Tip into the pastry shell and add dots of butter or margarine over the apple mixture.

Arrange the large pastry leaves in a decorative pattern on top, and decorate the edges with the smaller leaves. Mix the egg yolk with the cream and brush it over the leaves.

Bake in the preheated oven for 10 minutes. Reduce the oven temperature to 350°F. Cook for 35–45 minutes more until the pastry is golden brown. Allow the pie to cool in the pan slightly before removing it and putting it on a wire cooling rack.

TARTE TATIN

This delicious caramelized fruit tart from France was originally created by the Tatin sisters who ran a popular restaurant in Sologne in the Orléanais.

Serves 4

6 tablespoons butter, softened

6 tablespoons brown sugar,
  firmly packed

10 firm, sweet eating apples, peeled,
  cored and thickly sliced

whipped cream, to serve (optional)

For the pastry

4 tablespoons butter, softened

3 tablespoons superfine sugar

1 egg

1 cup flour

pinch of salt

COOK'S TIP

It is important to use firm apples for this tart so that they will hold their shape well during cooking. Any type of firm eating apples will be suitable.

To make the pastry, cream the butter and sugar in a bowl until pale and creamy. Beat in the egg, then sift in the flour and salt and mix to a soft dough. On a lightly floured surface, knead gently and bring together into a ball. Chill, covered or wrapped, for 1 hour.

Grease a 9-inch cake pan, then add 4 tablespoons of the butter. Place the cake pan on the burner and melt the butter gently. Remove and sprinkle over 4 tablespoons of the sugar.

Arrange the apple slices on top, then sprinkle with the remaining sugar and dot with the remaining butter.

Preheat the oven to 450°F. Place the cake pan on the burner again over a low to moderate heat for about 15 minutes, until a light golden caramel forms on the base. Remove the pan from the heat.

Roll out the pastry on a lightly floured surface to a round the same size as the pan and lay on top of the apples. Tuck the pastry edges down around the sides of the apples. Trim away any excess pastry.

Bake for about 20–25 minutes, until the pastry is golden brown. Remove the tart from the oven and let stand for about 5 minutes.

Place an upturned plate on top of the pan and, holding the two together with a dish towel, turn the apple tart out on to the plate. Serve while still warm with whipped cream, if wished.

DUTCH APPLE TART

Sliced almonds give this tart a wonderful crunchiness.

Serves 4–6
*6 eating apples, peeled, cored
    and grated*
4 tablespoons brown sugar
¼ teaspoon vanilla extract
½ teaspoon ground cinnamon
scant ¼ cup raisins
¼ cup sliced almonds, toasted
*1 tablespoon superfine sugar,
    for sprinkling*
whipped cream, to serve

For the pastry
1½ cups flour
*generous ½ cup butter, cubed
    and softened*
6 tablespoons superfine sugar
pinch of salt

Preheat the oven to 350°F. Lightly butter an 8-inch round springform pan and dust with a little flour.

To make the pastry, place the flour in a bowl with the butter and sugar, then squeeze together to form a firm dough. Knead lightly and bring together into a ball. Chill, covered or wrapped, for 1 hour.

Roll two-thirds of the chilled pastry out on a lightly floured surface to form a 10-inch round. Use this to line the base and two-thirds up the sides of the prepared pan, pressing the pastry up the sides with your fingers. Trim away any excess pastry.

Mix together the apples, sugar, vanilla extract, cinnamon, raisins, and almonds in a bowl. Spoon into the lined pan and level the surface. Fold the pastry edge above the level of the apples down over the filling.

Roll out the remaining pastry and cut into eight ½-inch strips. Brush the strips with cold water and sprinkle over the superfine sugar. Lay the strips on top of the tart in a lattice pattern, securing the ends to the folded-over edge with water.

Bake in the center of the oven for 1 hour, or until the pastry is golden brown. Remove and let cool in the pan. When the tart is cold, carefully remove it from the pan. Serve cut into slices with whipped cream.

APPLE MERINGUE TART

Like pears, quinces substitute well in most apple recipes and are quick and delicious. If you ever find any quinces, this is the ideal tart to use them in.

Serves 6

1½ pounds eating apples

juice of ½ lemon

2 tablespoons butter

4 tablespoons raw sugar

cream or ice cream, to serve

For the pastry

½ cup flour

¾ cup whole-wheat flour

pinch of salt

½ cup superfine sugar

6 tablespoons butter

1 egg, separated, plus 1 egg white

To make the pastry, sift the flours into a bowl with the salt, adding in the wheat flakes from the sifter. Add 1 tablespoon of the superfine sugar and rub in the butter until the mixture forms soft crumbs.

Work in the egg yolk and, if necessary, 1–2 tablespoons cold water. Knead lightly and bring together into a ball. Chill, covered or wrapped, for between 10 and 20 minutes.

Preheat the oven to 375°F. Roll the chilled pastry out on a lightly floured surface to form a 9-inch round and use to line an 8-inch pie pan. Line with wax paper and fill with baking beans. Bake blind for 15 minutes, then remove the paper and beans and cook for 5–10 minutes more, until the pastry is crisp and golden.

Meanwhile, peel, core, and slice the apples, then toss in lemon juice. Melt the butter, add the raw sugar and fry the apple until golden and just tender. Arrange in the pastry shell.

Preheat the oven to 425°F. Whisk the egg white until it is stiff. Whisk in half the remaining superfine sugar, then carefully fold in the rest. Pipe the meringue over the apples. Bake for 6–7 minutes. Serve the tart hot or cold with cream or ice cream.

APPLE AND PEAR SKILLET CAKE

This unusual cake, lightly spiced with cinnamon and nutmeg and baked in a frying pan, is impressively simple to make. It is delicious served hot.

Serves 6

1 apple, peeled, cored and thinly sliced

1 pear, peeled, cored and thinly sliced

½ cup walnut pieces, chopped

1 teaspoon ground cinnamon

1 teaspoon grated nutmeg

3 eggs

¾ cup flour

2 tablespoons brown sugar,
  firmly packed

¾ cup milk

1 teaspoon vanilla extract

4 tablespoons butter or margarine

confectioner's sugar, for sprinkling

cream or ice cream, to serve (optional)

Preheat the oven to 375°F. In a large bowl, toss together the apple slices, pear slices, walnuts, cinnamon, and nutmeg until thoroughly combined. Set aside.

With an electric mixer, beat together the eggs, flour, brown sugar, milk, and vanilla extract. Melt the butter or margarine in a 9- or 10-inch ovenproof frying pan (preferably cast-iron) over moderate heat. Add the apple mixture and cook for about 5 minutes, until it is lightly caramelized, stirring occasionally. When cooked, make sure that the apple and pear mixture is evenly distributed in the frying pan.

Pour the sponge mixture over the fruit and nuts. Transfer the skillet to the preheated oven and bake for about 30 minutes, until the cake is puffy and pulls away from the sides of the pan. Serve hot sprinkled with confectioner's sugar, with cream or ice cream as an accompaniment, if you wish.

COOK'S TIP
This cake should be served straight from the frying pan. There is no need to transfer it to a serving plate first.

CRANBERRY AND APPLE RING

Tangy cranberries add an unusual flavor to this light-textured cake. It is best eaten very fresh.

Serves 4–6

2 cups self-rising flour

1 teaspoon ground cinnamon

6 tablespoons brown sugar

1 crisp eating apple, cored and diced

⅔ cup fresh or frozen cranberries

4 tablespoons sunflower oil

⅔ cup apple juice

cranberry jelly and apple slices,
*   to decorate*

Preheat the oven to 350°F. Lightly grease a 4-cup ring pan with oil. It is easiest to do this with a pastry brush, or you could use a paper towel.

Sift together the flour and ground cinnamon, then stir in the sugar. Toss together the diced apple and cranberries. Stir the fruit into the dry ingredients, then add the sunflower oil and apple juice and beat well until thoroughly combined.

Spoon the cake mixture into the prepared ring pan and bake in the preheated oven for about 35–40 minutes, or until the cake is firm to the touch. Turn the cake out and let cool completely on a wire cooling rack.

Just before serving, warm the cranberry jelly in a small saucepan over gentle heat. Decorate the top of the ring with the prepared apple slices, then drizzle the warmed cranberry jelly over the apple pieces, letting it run down the sides of the ring.

COOK'S TIP
Fresh cranberries are readily available throughout the winter months and if you don't use them all at once, they can be frozen for up to a year.

APPLE CRUMBLE CAKE

A rich and filling cake which is excellent served with thick cream or custard.

Serves 8–10

For the topping
¾ cup self-rising flour
½ teaspoon ground cinnamon
3 tablespoons butter
2 tablespoons sugar

For the base
4 tablespoons butter, softened
6 tablespoons sugar
1 large egg, beaten
1 cup self-rising flour, sifted
2 firm, tart cooking apples (about
  1 pound), peeled, cored and sliced
⅓ cup golden raisins

To decorate
1 red eating apple, cored, thinly sliced
  and tossed in lemon juice
2 tablespoons superfine sugar, sifted
pinch of ground cinnamon

Preheat the oven to 350°F. Lightly grease and line a deep 7-inch springform pan.

To make the topping, sift the flour and cinnamon together into a bowl. Rub in the butter until the mixture forms soft crumbs, then stir in the sugar. Set aside until needed.

To make the base for the cake, put the butter, sugar, egg, and flour into a bowl and beat for 1–2 minutes until smooth. Spoon into the prepared pan and even out the surface.

Mix together the apple slices and golden raisins and spread them evenly over the top of the base. Sprinkle with the topping.

Bake in the center of the preheated oven for about 1 hour. Then remove from the oven and cool in the pan for 10 minutes before turning out on to a wire cooling rack and peeling off the lining paper. Serve warm or cool, decorated with the prepared slices of red eating apple, and with sugar and cinnamon sprinkled over the top.

Hot Desserts

Apples make a perfect addition to warming desserts,

delicate sponges and hearty, satisfying crumbles;

or try them caramelized in a deliciously sweet and

sticky toffee-flavored pudding.

CARAMELIZED APPLES

A sweet, sticky dessert which is very quickly made, and usually very quickly eaten!

Serves 4

1½ pounds eating apples

½ cup sweet butter

1 ounce fresh white bread crumbs

½ cup ground almonds

finely grated rind of 2 lemons

4 tablespoons corn syrup

4 tablespoons clotted cream,
   to serve

COOK'S TIP

*The easiest and quickest way to
make bread crumbs is to put
slices of bread into a food
processor or blender. Coarsely
chop the bread for several
seconds until crumbs form. Take
care not to overchop.*

Peel and core the apples. Carefully cut the apples into ½-inch thick rings. Heat a wok and add the butter. When the butter has melted, add the apple rings and stir-fry for 4 minutes until golden and tender. Remove from the wok, reserving the butter. Add the bread crumbs to the hot butter and stir-fry for 1 minute.

Stir in the ground almonds and lemon rind and stir-fry for 3 minutes more, stirring constantly. Sprinkle the bread crumb mix over the apples, then drizzle warmed corn syrup over the top. Serve with the cream.

EVE'S PUDDING

This pudding is irresistible! The tempting, tender apples beneath the rich sponge topping are the reason for its name.

Serves 4–6

½ cup butter

½ cup superfine sugar

2 eggs, beaten

grated rind and juice of 1 lemon

scant 1 cup self-rising flour

⅓ cup ground almonds

scant ½ cup brown sugar

3 firm, tart cooking apples (about 1½ pounds), cored and thinly sliced

¼ cup sliced almonds

whipped cream, to serve

Beat together the butter and superfine sugar in a large bowl until the mixture is very light and fluffy.

Gradually beat the eggs into the butter mixture, beating well after each addition, then fold in the lemon rind, flour, and ground almonds.

Mix together the brown sugar, apples, and lemon juice, turn into the dish, and level out. Add the sponge mixture, then the almonds. Bake for 40–45 minutes, until golden. Serve warm with whipped cream.

CHUNKY APPLE BAKE

This filling, economical family dessert is a good way to use up slightly stale bread – any type of bread will do, but whole wheat is richest in fiber.

Serves 4

2 firm, tart cooking apples (about
  1 pound)
3 ounces whole wheat bread,
  without crusts
½ cup cottage cheese
3 tablespoons brown sugar
⅞ cup low-fat milk
1 teaspoon demerara sugar

COOK'S TIP
You may need to adjust the amount of milk used, depending on the dryness of the bread; the staler the bread, the more milk it will absorb.

reheat the oven to 425°F. Peel the apples, cut them in quarters, and remove the cores.

Roughly chop the apples into even-size pieces, about ½ inch across. Cut the bread into ½-inch dice.

Toss together the apples, bread, cottage cheese, and sugar. Stir in the milk and then spoon the mixture into a wide ovenproof dish. Sprinkle with the demerara sugar.

Bake for 30–35 minutes, or until golden brown and bubbling. Serve hot.

APPLE AND KUMQUAT SPONGE PUDDINGS

The kumquats provide a surprising tanginess in this dessert.

Serves 8

generous ½ cup butter, at room
   temperature

6 ounces firm, tart cooking apples,
   peeled and thinly sliced

3 ounces kumquats, thinly sliced

generous ½ cup superfine sugar

2 eggs

1 cup self-rising flour

For the sauce

3 ounces kumquats, thinly sliced

6 tablespoons superfine sugar

1 cup water

⅔ cup crème fraîche

1 teaspoon cornstarch mixed with
   2 teaspoons water

lemon juice, to taste

Prepare the steamer. Lightly butter eight ⅔-cup dariole molds or ramekins and put a disc of buttered waxed paper on the base of each one.

Melt 2 tablespoons butter in a frying pan. Add the apples, kumquats, and 2 tablespoons sugar and cook over a moderate heat for 5–8 minutes or until the apples start to soften and the sugar begins to caramelize. Remove from the heat and let cool.

Meanwhile, cream the remaining butter with the remaining sugar until the mixture is pale and fluffy. Add the eggs, one at a time, beating well after each addition. Fold in the flour.

Divide the apple and kumquat mixture among the prepared molds. Top with the sponge mixture. Cover the molds and put them into the steamer. Steam on top of the burner for 45 minutes.

To make the sauce, put the kumquats, sugar, and water in a frying pan and bring to a boil, stirring to dissolve the sugar. Simmer for 5 minutes. Stir in the crème fraîche and bring back to a boil, stirring.

Remove from the heat and whisk in the cornstarch mixture. Return the pan to the heat and simmer gently for 2 minutes more, stirring constantly. Add lemon juice to taste. Turn out the puddings and serve hot with the kumquat sauce.

APPLE COUSCOUS PUDDING

This unusual couscous mixture makes a delicious dessert with a rich, fruity flavor, but virtually no fat.

Serves 4

2½ cups apple juice

⅔ cup couscous

¼ cup raisins

½ teaspoon mixed spice

1 large tart, firm cooking apple, peeled,
   cored and sliced

2 tablespoons raw sugar

plain low-fat yogurt, to serve

Preheat the oven to 400°F. Place the apple juice, couscous, raisins, and spice in a pan and bring to a boil, stirring. Cover and simmer for 10–12 minutes, until all the free liquid is absorbed.

Spoon half the couscous mixture into a 5-cup ovenproof dish and top with half the apple slices. Top with the remaining couscous.

Arrange the remaining apple slices overlapping over the top and sprinkle with raw sugar. Bake in the oven for 25–30 minutes, or until golden brown. Serve hot with yogurt.

COOK'S TIP

*To ring the changes, substitute
other dried fruits for the raisins
in this recipe – try chopped dates
or ready-to-eat pears, figs,
peaches, or apricots.*

APPLE AND BLACKBERRY NUT CRUMBLE

This much-loved dish is perhaps one of the simplest and most delicious of traditional hot desserts.

Serves 4

*4 firm, tart cooking apples (about
  2 pounds), peeled, cored and sliced*
½ cup butter, cubed
⅝ cup brown sugar, firmly packed
1¾ cups blackberries

For the topping
¾ cup whole wheat flour
¾ cup flour
½ teaspoon ground cinnamon
*3 tablespoons chopped mixed
  nuts, toasted*
custard, cream, or ice cream, to serve

Preheat the oven to 350°F. Lightly butter a 5-cup ovenproof dish. Place the apples in a pan with 2 tablespoons of the butter, 2 tablespoons of the sugar, and 1 tablespoon water. Cover and cook gently for about 10 minutes, until just tender. Remove from the heat and gently stir in the blackberries. Spoon the mixture into the dish and set aside.

To make the crumble topping, sift the flours and cinnamon into a bowl (tip in any of the wheat flakes left in the sifter). Add the remaining 6 tablespoons butter and rub into the flour with your fingertips until the mixture resembles fine crumbs (or you can use a food processor or blender).

Stir in the remaining 6 tablespoons sugar and the nuts and mix well. Sprinkle the crumble topping over the fruit. Bake for 35–40 minutes, until the top is golden brown. Serve hot with custard, cream, or ice cream.

APPLE CHARLOTTE

This classic dessert takes its name from the straight-sided pan with heart-shaped handles in which it is baked. The buttery bread crust encases a thick, sweet, yet sharp apple purée.

Serves 6

5 firm, tart cooking apples (about 2½ pounds)

2 tablespoons water

generous ½ cup brown sugar

½ teaspoon ground cinnamon

¼ teaspoon ground nutmeg

7 slices firm, textured sliced white bread

5–6 tablespoons butter, melted

custard, to serve (optional)

COOK'S TIP

If preferred, microwave the apples without water in a large glass dish on High (100% power), tightly covered, for 15 minutes. Add the sugar and spices and microwave, uncovered, for about 15 minutes more until very thick, stirring once or twice.

Peel, quarter, and core the apples. Cut into thick slices and put in a large heavy-based pan with the water. Cook, covered, over a moderate heat for 5 minutes, and then uncover the pan and cook for 10 minutes until the apples are very soft. Add the sugar, cinnamon, and nutmeg and continue cooking for 5–10 minutes, stirring frequently, until the apples are soft and thick. (There should be about 3 cups of apple purée.)

Preheat the oven to 400°F. Trim the crusts from the bread and brush with melted butter on one side. Cut two slices into triangles and use as many as necessary to cover the base of a 6-cup charlotte pan or soufflé dish, placing the bread triangles buttered-side down and fitting them tightly. Cut the fingers of bread the same height as the pan or dish and use them to line the sides completely, overlapping them slightly and making sure there are no gaps.

Pour the apple purée into the pan or dish. Cover the top with bread slices, buttered-side up, cutting them as necessary to fit.

Bake the charlotte for 20 minutes. Reduce the oven temperature to 350°F and bake for 25 minutes more until golden brown and firm. Let stand for 15 minutes. To turn out, place a serving plate over the pan or dish. Using a dish towel, hold tightly, and invert, then lift off the pan or dish. Serve with hot custard, if wished.

BAKED APPLES WITH CARAMEL SAUCE

The creamy caramel sauce adds a touch of sophistication to this traditional dish.

Serves 6

*3 Granny Smith apples, cored but
  not peeled*

*3 Red Delicious apples, cored but
  not peeled*

³/4 cup brown sugar, firmly packed

³/4 cup water

¹/2 teaspoon grated nutmeg

*¹/4 teaspoon ground
  black pepper*

¹/4 cup walnut pieces

¹/4 cup golden raisins

*4 tablespoons butter or
  margarine, diced*

For the caramel sauce

1 tablespoon butter or margarine

¹/2 cup whipping cream

COOK'S TIP

*Use a mixture of firm red and
gold pears instead of the apples.
Cook for 10 minutes longer.*

Preheat the oven to 375°F. Lightly grease a baking pan. With a small knife, enlarge the core opening at the stem end of each apple to about 1 inch in diameter. Arrange the apples in the pan, stem end up.

In a small pan, combine the brown sugar, water, nutmeg, and pepper. Boil the mixture, stirring, for 6 minutes. Mix together the walnuts and golden raisins. Spoon some of the walnut mixture into each apple. Top with some diced butter or margarine. Spoon the sugar sauce over and around the apples. Bake, basting occasionally, until the apples are just tender, about 50 minutes. Put the apples in a serving dish, reserving the sauce in the baking dish. Keep the apples warm.

To make the caramel sauce, mix the butter or margarine, cream, and reserved sauce in a pan. Bring to a boil, stirring, and simmer for 2 minutes until thickened. Let the sauce cool slightly before serving.

APPLE SOUFFLE OMELET

Apples sautéed until they are slightly caramelized make a delicious seasonal filling for sweet omelets.

Serves 2

4 eggs, separated

2 tablespoons light cream

1 tablespoon superfine sugar

1 tablespoon butter

confectioner's sugar, for dredging

For the filling

2 tablespoons butter

2 tablespoons brown sugar

1 eating apple, peeled, cored
* and sliced*

3 tablespoons light cream

To make the filling, heat the butter and sugar in a frying pan and sauté the apple slices until just tender. Stir in the cream and keep warm.

Place the egg yolks in a bowl with the cream and sugar and beat well. Whisk the egg whites until stiff, then fold into the yolk mixture.

Melt the butter in a large heavy-based frying pan, pour in the soufflé mixture and spread evenly. Cook for 1 minute until golden underneath, then place under a hot broiler to brown the top.

Slide the omelet on to a plate, add the apple mixture, then fold over. Sift the confectioner's sugar over thickly, then mark in a criss-cross pattern with a hot metal skewer. Serve immediately.

Cold Desserts

For a special occasion meal, tart, fresh apples make a

fabulous finale when combined with roasted hazelnuts

in a crisp, layered shortcake, and with blackberries

in two spectacular iced desserts.

BLACKBERRY AND APPLE ROMANOFF

Rich yet fruity, this dessert is popular with most people and very quick to make.

Serves 6–8

*3–4 sharp eating apples, peeled, cored
   and chopped*

3 tablespoons superfine sugar

1 cup whipping cream

1 teaspoon grated lemon rind

6 tablespoons strained plain yogurt

*4–6 crisp meringues (about 2 ounces),
   coarsely crumbled*

8 ounces fresh or frozen blackberries

*whipped cream, a few blackberries,
   and mint leaves, to decorate*

COOK'S TIP

*This also makes a delicious ice
cream, though the texture of the
frozen berries makes it difficult
to scoop if it is frozen for more
than 4–6 hours.*

With plastic wrap, line a 4–5-cup pudding bowl. Toss the apples into a pan with 2 tablespoons of the sugar and cook for 2–3 minutes, or until softening. Mash the apples with a fork and let cool.

Whip the cream and fold in the lemon rind, yogurt, the remaining sugar, the apples, and the crumbled meringues.

Gently stir in the blackberries, then tip the mixture into the pudding bowl and freeze for 1–3 hours.

Turn out on to a plate and remove the plastic wrap. Serve decorated with piped cream, blackberries, and mint leaves.

APPLE AND HAZELNUT SHORTCAKE

This variation of a traditional recipe will be popular with all the family.

Serves 8–10

1 cup whole wheat flour

4 tablespoons ground hazelnuts

*4 tablespoons confectioner's
  sugar, sifted*

*10 tablespoons sweet butter
  or margarine*

3 sharp eating apples

1 teaspoon lemon juice

about 1–2 tablespoons sugar, to taste

*1 tablespoon chopped fresh mint, or
  1 teaspoon dried*

1 cup whipping cream or crème fraîche

few drops of vanilla extract

*few mint leaves and whole hazelnuts,
  to decorate*

Process the flour, ground hazelnuts, and confectioner's sugar with the butter in a food processor or blender in short bursts, or rub the butter into the dry ingredients until they come together into a ball. (Don't overwork the mixture.) Add a very little iced water if necessary. Knead briefly, then chill, covered or wrapped, for about 30 minutes.

Preheat the oven to 325°F. Cut the chilled dough in half and roll out each half, on a lightly floured surface, to form a 7-inch round. Place the rounds on wax paper on baking sheets and bake for about 40 minutes, or until crisp. If the shortcakes are browning too much, move them down in the oven to a lower shelf. Allow to cool.

Peel, core, and chop the apples into a pan with the lemon juice. Add sugar to taste, then cook for about 2–3 minutes, until just softening. Mash the apple gently with the chopped fresh mint and let cool.

Whip the cream or crème fraîche with the vanilla extract. Place one shortcake round on a serving plate. Carefully spread half the apple and then half the cream or crème fraîche on top of the shortcake.

Place the second shortcake on top, then spread over the remaining apple and cream, swirling the top layer of cream gently. Serve immediately decorated with mint leaves and a few whole hazelnuts.

FROZEN APPLE AND BLACKBERRY TERRINE

Apples and blackberries are a classic seasonal combination; they really complement each other. This pretty, three-layered terrine can be frozen, so you can enjoy it at any time of year.

Serves 6

*2 cooking or eating apples (about
   1 pound)*
1¼ cups cider
1 tablespoon clear honey
1 teaspoon vanilla extract
*scant 2 cups fresh or frozen
   blackberries, thawed*
1 packet powdered gelatin
2 egg whites
*fresh apple slices and blackberries,
   to decorate*

COOK'S TIP

*For a quicker version, set the
mixture without layering. Purée
the fruit together, stir in the
dissolved gelatin and whisked
egg whites, turn into the pan
and let set.*

Peel, core, and chop the apples and place them in a pan, with half the cider. Bring the cider to a boil, then cover the pan and let the apples simmer gently until tender.

Turn the apples into a food processor or blender and process to a smooth purée. Stir in the honey and vanilla. Add half the blackberries to half the apple purée. Process again until smooth. Strain to remove the seeds.

Heat the remaining cider until it is almost boiling, and then sprinkle the gelatin over and stir until the gelatin has completely dissolved. Add half the gelatin mixture to the apple purée and half to the blackberry purée.

Let the purées cool until almost set. Whisk the egg whites until they are stiff. Quickly fold them into the apple purée. Remove half the purée to another bowl. Stir the remaining whole blackberries into half the apple purée, and then turn this into a 7½-cup loaf pan, packing it down firmly.

Top with the blackberry purée and spread it evenly. Finally, add a layer of the apple purée and smooth it evenly. If necessary, freeze each layer until firm before adding the next.

Freeze until firm. To serve, allow to stand at room temperature for about 20 minutes to soften, and then cut into slices, decorated with the fresh apple slices and some blackberries.

INDEX

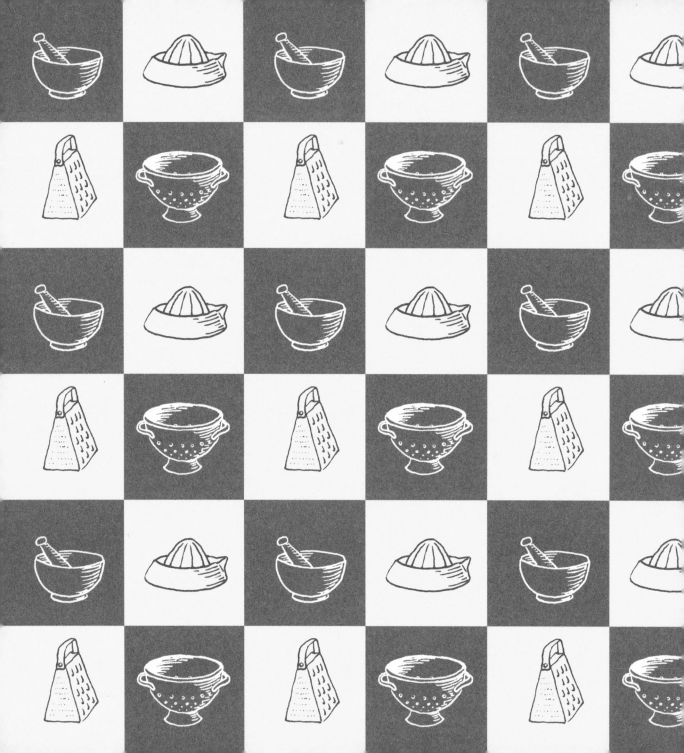